We Follow the River

Caitlin Press Inc.
3375 Ponderosa Way
Qualicum Beach, BC V9K 2J8
www.caitlinpress.com

Text design by Vici Johnstone
Cover design by Onjana Yawnghwe and Vici Johnstone
Cover artwork by Sawangwongse Yawnghwe

Printed in Canada

Caitlin Press Inc. acknowledges financial support from the Government of Canada and the Canada Council for the Arts, and the Province of British Columbia through the British Columbia Arts Council and the Book Publisher's Tax Credit.

Library and Archives Canada Cataloguing in Publication

We follow the river / Onjana Yawnghwe.
Yawnghwe, Onjana, author.
Poems.
Canadiana 20230528449 | ISBN 9781773861388 (softcover)
LCC PS8647.A78 W4 2024 | DDC C811/.6-dc23

WE FOLLOW THE RIVER

POEMS

Onjana Yawnghwe

Caitlin Press 2024

*In memory of Nu Nu and
Chao Tzang Yawnghwe.*

Contents

A

B

C

A

Memories are
      not enough
for words
to hold on.

      The mind shifts
finding new footing,
      new ground.

Mountains where
      once was jungle.

English: a concrete building.

      I see through
its windows.

            Myself reflected.

BRAID

Even with hands
    cracked from cleaning

still she beckons me
    to sit by her lap

        amidst the sound of cars rushing
        past the hum of evergreens
        and mountains that loom
        over our small apartment.

She begins to braid
    humming Connie Francis tunes

but only later do I wonder
    what she dreamed of.

        If she longed for late afternoons
        when geckoes begin to appear
        when the air is draped with mangoes
        and reckless chirrups.

Her fingers dreamed forests for me
as her hands twist and pull hard
    so that I wouldn't break.

        Under her palms I fall
        under the tops of trees
            into warmth and spice and waving sunlight
            into memories of green and sky
            and a land where she fits.

Through the tough pull
and tug of hair

bare and strong
her hands tumble
me into her sarong.

My Mother's Hands

All she has is a bare-bone life
all bent and swollen fingers.

The knuckling down
      the leaving and arriving.

The nothing much to hold on to
but flinty, broken hope
        wrapped in torn paper tissue.

      Surrounded by whiteness—
this mountain-turned air—

      Here.

          Time hurries and stumbles.
Wind chills and clouds loom.
This land unforgiving to tropical hands.

Who to understand
her orange light.

        Who to carry her life
            and take it gently from
                her spotted hands.

CROSSINGS

Between us

  words
  rocks

      your arms start to falter.

      They are too heavy.

      (We fall into oceans.)

            ✺

A friend says that sons and daughters
somehow carry the tragedies of their parents.

            Written on their hands
            loss is passed on

(what are mother and father but
            loss unnamed).

For the country
      they have given up

            for the waters crossed
            for the poverty of the brand new
            for time, uncertain, wavering on a pin.

The river carries it all.
The burdens.
The heavy heart.
Always filling
always emptying.

AIRPLANE MAN

My dad a former pack-a-day man
now savours just a few cigarettes
he delicately breaks in half
inhaling with religious fervency.

I'm vigilant, check that he doesn't buy
too many bottles   hide too many cartons.

When he pours himself a glass I'm fearful it will lead
to two or more   to him veering off   losing control
I want him on stable ground   on placid earth but he's not
that kind of man   he makes his own history
his mind ready to flame   his temper a force
effective for politics   for the fight for Burma
but   too much   for the thin walls of home.

෧

Over the years he's mellowed some
body rounded   teeth frail and nicotine-stained
still working for the cause he's since lost hope for.

He denies martyrs and miracle workers.
But those pesky ideals stay with him.

His feet still don't stay on the ground

      they're in the air

           crossing continents—

SCAR

For years he stays silent about
　　　that long pink mountain range
　　　　　knitted across the skin of his chest.

I often mistake his silence for anger
　　　as one of the many things never spoken
many things with other lives other lands.

But when he finally opens up
it's with the Thai backbeat of gunfire—
a goddamn gunshot from nowhere
but it turned out that the bastard was
on the back of a motorcycle imagine
I was on the motorcycle too can you believe it
swerved into the ditch to save myself
shit the bullet just passed my heart was close
to dying and not only that we didn't have
good doctors back then so I almost
died on the operation slab dead and done

Later I get another story from mom—
no, it's from an operation that he'd had 'cause
he was born with a congenital heart defect
that's why he never travelled as a boy
or go off to boarding schools to India or England
like your uncles and aunts that's why
he's less British than the others and
that's how he met and married me
but what're you making that face for
it's true he was actually shot at in Thailand
he was on a motorcycle and drove into
the ditch but it was his friend who'd
sat at the back of the bike who was shot
they were trying to kill your dad though
but his friend didn't survive just died on the spot

❧

In Thailand he'd kept a handgun in a
        shiny red suitcase by his bedside.

                When scars come
                how does one know
                if they've healed
                or just covering up pain
                like blindfold to eye.

If silence is a scar

what wound lies beneath.

❧

In all these years

I'd never thought

he had a weak heart.

HER, COOKING

In the wok
onions sliced transparent
hiss loose electricity
jump-dance like popcorn
fire-wired skin stained turmeric
saffron monks' robes holy Buddhist days
paprika underlayer dug dried by the sun
                oh her fingers will stay yellow

Her breasts rub thin fabric of shirt
as she stirs crumbling tuah noa yes
we celebrate rotten soybeans crushed dried
      it explodes in the pan
      it erupts in full force
sewer-sour pungent
      a mouth-watering goddess emerges in full orange batiks
        swinging her hips like a word on a Bangkok street

By the time leaky tomatoes join the dance
      people on roads mysteriously quicken their strides
        as nam pla nudges footprints before them

Boiled long-strand rice noodles
boiled pig's blood in gelatinous bricks
      deep red dust hot hit
pile of parachute limes sliced into
          spectacular sour

Every pore of skin

      becomes

   nose
      swells
                 tongue
               spreads

   mouth
     falling

           open

GREEN MANGO

A mango is good orange runny and sweet
sweet so your skin is marinated golden and
fingers and mouth invite another's tongue
to lick, lick, suck, sweet candy. Yum.
Good on summer days when sweat
makes brown skin sticky, sticky but salty
salty and sweet like Chinese take-out:
take a red-bathed shrimp and close your eyes
pretend you're a giant eating a curled limb. Yum.
Those days when you just have to laugh
at each other's faces, all orange and salty
with red-stained mouths, 'cause there's
nothing else to do but maybe lick.

If you go to Indiantown or Chinatown
look around between stooping bobbing
heads, through waving limbs, below raised voices
you see red and yellow and hairy brown
but look for green, round, tapering at the end.
A nice weight, good to juggle, heavy.
Not red or yellow or the colour in between. Green.
Hard. Between stone and grapefruit—
the closer to stone the better, don't let colour deceive you.
Many times I've succumbed to green and just firmness,
skipping open my front door and muttering in glee:
"Green mango, green mango, green mango!"
only to peel off skin and see ripe yellow
so you can't tell, even if it is green and hard,
whether it is a real, authentic green mango.
Or not.

Let those slept-in soft ones warm
yellow to red in their blushing skins.
Hold these young green ones, hard and sincere
place them to your nose.
If you come from a faraway place maybe you'll remember it.
Remember this is what green smells like,
this is what fresh is, this is another home.
Sticky from sap, wash them under running water
peel them gently, as thin-skin as possible
throw the peel over your shoulder—it might spell
the name of your true love—though not in English.

Push knife straight down white meat.
Cut through the still soft seed, wedge the flesh,
dip in salt in sauce or brave it plain
lay it firm, poking tongue, touching teeth.
Keer-rawp! Ker-rawp! Crunch, crunch,
until your head is stupefied with crunch, sour, salt,
again and your tongue brightens in attack
and your mouth fills with water and your
ears and mouth are full, teeth a-battle
so all you hear is thick, thick thunder,
banging your eardrum so much so
that it's all you know of this place
all you know of where you came from
all you know of welcome and coming home
all you know of where you are and will be—
distilled in a sharp firm slice of green.

EVENING PRAYER

Between sleep and dream
from the pull of mouth muscle
the twitch of tongue,
into the hum of throat,
down to the column,
solid heart, of self

                    Buddha saranam gacchami

The nights we climbed
into mom's bed
sleep tip-toeing

                    Dhammam saranam gacchami

we would repeat until
the lone-lamped room
rose and filled with
level, deep rumblings
of a language we lost
and didn't understand

Mouths memorising
mouth-shapes

                    Sangham saranam gachhami

Remember not the meaning
but the feeling of those words

        for the space they open

        into cloud and blue sky

        like a breeze combing back

        to loosen strands of your hair.

MOVING EARTH

I crack earth open with a shovel
a rain-sunk mound crusted over
slow hard-baking in ovened summer;
the taste of rain in the wind, the sky
turns over, distending its grey belly
wide touching the ragged tips of mountains.

I hear the sharp slicing of metal
bend down and upturn my scoopful:
as if the soil is frosting up eggs
the ground bubbles with rocks—
a few fist-heavy, numerous smaller
all sprout up greeting air.

I stop for a moment, realising how hard
it will be to make my mother a garden.

She spends forever leaving home.
She needs this narrow piece of land
to know one armful of earth is for her.

She witnesses Burma change from white-gloved
British hands meticulously picking rubies from the land
to clouded Japanese faces drooping with hunger and war
to the confused, brutal fists of her countrymen
all rebel-hungry and wanting
and the land is squeezed starving by men
who cling to guns with one hand
and cover their eyes with the other
so they won't see what their army boots
and trigger fingers are doing.

The country is shut off.
Blood everywhere.

Her hands too are soaked in blood
she, my father, and the exhausted people
the government thought they'd beaten
down rust-coloured mud fight back.
But nothing changes, smallness raised
against enormity is ground down.
She escapes to Thailand and mimes a life;
comes to Canada and does the same.

Kneeling on the loosened earth,
    my hands enter coolness.

I shift one handful of dirt
    to another, sifting stones.

Rocks pant as they rub each other.

The damp smell of shaded trees
    wind breathing round branches—
        the old years of being here.

It's been a long time
since I've touched earth.

Six years old, I dig just for digging,
not with sharp metal but with sticks
and with fingernails, hard and tanned
I discover the colours of the land:

Chiang Mai in my backyard,
the ground is dust, a yellow that doesn't shine
and hands are powdered in an instant
and yellow turns molten gold in hot palms.

Deeper, earth becomes wetter and cooler,
clay redder and denser than chili paste.
My skin is finger-painted fire
I taste it to see if it would burn
but my mouth grows sudden cool and
I'm in a cave, smelling wet, rain, rock.
I rub my lips with red and become beautiful
that instant ready to be a woman even though
I'm still a girl I'll hold to my chest bleeding
rubies bursting from lips and fingertips.

Next layer is like death
dark brown, almost black:
the cold of cut bones.
I dig and dig and it never ends.

I am afraid to touch it.
I stare at the small hole:
yellow, red, then black.

Blackness pushes under my fingernails
    dampness floods beneath my skin.
I push open more soil, heavy persuasion:
        more stones like baby potatoes burst up
        coated with coarse and moist darkness.

The smell of slowness covers everything
penetrates my palms and fingers into rivers.

    All things natural must smell like this
of soil, bark, rotten fruit, rain and even clouds
        of night with its heart-rounding scent of closeness
            of long faded stars which loiter still clinging to bodies
        the vague stinging salt of the sea patting cheeks red
            exuding from coupled-skins in close-clasping darkness.

    This odour of permanence, of always being.

Wispy-thin roots tangle in earth,
sprouts like winding roads gleam pure white,
nuggets of red cedar nestle, some lined and rotting,
some whittled down in dirt to a whirling top,
some spare and dry as ocean driftwood bleached pale,
some mimicking a scrap of human spine.
Armoured insects no bigger than a point on a page
swiftly scramble between hollows of soil, up
spider-legged moss, hairy wet and moulded yellow
while one thin red worm coils itself into a knot
while another stretches out bloated and heavy
mottled purple squirms up S-shapes as I shovel
all this up and lay it over new, level ground.

I am expecting waist-deep snow so cold it burns
that's what I was hoping for but this is Vancouver
and it happens to be August and the streets are grey
not white and hard with sun and the concrete rasps.

We live in a three-part beige apartment complex
in Mount Pleasant and I don't talk to anybody
because I'm afraid and I can't speak English or
even smile in English but I learn quick and those
little girls ask me why my lips are so huge my nose
so flat why so beady eyes and all the while I'm expecting snow.
Mom works all day first at McDonald's then as a housekeeper
and she's no longer a schoolteacher instead she
cleans people's toilets and mops floors
wet rags in her hands, knees touching tile.

We only touch concrete grey and pass by grass
growing in rectangles along sidewalks and they rise
in brittle yellow points and threaten holes in our feet;
sometimes we see hand-stretching roses or dahlias
which are always mysteriously bright pink.
I like dandelions which grow free and spontaneous
in places people don't want them to, and they beam
like shaken suns, globe-change quickly and I help them
blow away by vigorously kicking them airborne and
watch seeds like parachuting snowflakes
search for a bit of land to make a home on
to ground down roots that will stick no matter
how many people try to pull them out.

Earth remembers hands that touch it,
that stroke its curves and curl against its body,
that caress its fine hair of roots and petal-lips,
that gently part open its ankles, knees and thighs,
cleaving soft fluffy soil with two palms pressed
      and bury a snowflake which quickly disappears
            down past rocks, worms, and bone-shaped wood.

It recalls the abrupt depressions of flesh,
      of nameless bodies collapsing in reddened mud
      of them who vanish suddenly from homes
who spend their last few seconds cradled by this soil.

Of them who remain behind to remember.

Her voice low and slow, breathing in music,
she tells me of Shan State, how it wore chill by day,
not the sun-flamed robes of the sweltering south,
how raw mist would ride over the valley and lag
leaving skin glistening like it'd been dipped in stars.
Of certain leaves which taste bitter against your teeth
but soon a sweetness lingers softly round the tongue,
so you only recall the mouth-filling sugar of longing.

How the cold-tinged air hangs slow with jasmine,
white blossoms as large as her father's hands,
so many she can hardly see green within;
how her fingers pick the flowers,
gently until they release themselves into
her clay bowl, so large and earth-heavy
she has to stretch wide her small embrace,
hugging smells to her skin with thin arms.

Between her words, the roll and tumble of them
the way they come out singing the same song
             her memories drop like rice before my feet
Shan mountain breath in my ear.
From her hair the smell of rust and earth
the scent of blood she'd held in her hands
        the tongue hidden beneath the soil
        the dream the darkness in her eyes
an amazon of leaves gleaming blackness,
her body the moist naked ground.

Roots gather at the fall
and touch of her words.

I dream mango trees are growing in my backyard
drooping heavy with fruit stubbornly sour-hard.
Tall banana trees sprout up crunchy and green
their arms glossing light and flapping like flags—
        at earth-level, round mushrooms like black pebbles
             murmur beneath tree-shade, nesting in silky soil—
I eat them again, dropping them raw into my mouth
        each mushroom-marble pops between my teeth
             and I'm eating firecrackers and earth, in my cheeks
                 stones drop into a well of water in moonlight
                     echo off my teeth and plunge down my throat.

I dream of so many things.

Grip stones.

      Touch water.

Heaviness enters my warm fist.

Stones drag cool my blood.
 Air weaves through fingers
    swirls in palms even as
        my hand is gripping tight.

        I hold a forest iced by night
        the breath of northern seas
        stroking beyond the horizon
        steady moon-shadows gliding
        across light-brindled Inle Lake.

I wait for my fist to
warm the stones.

They stay cool
    long after
        my patience
runs out.

Skies stoop low, the air simmers
oceans roll in clouds as grey trembles—
rain falls as I step under a nearby tree.
The pile of stones shiver as a push of wind
runs through the branches, shaking from its leaves
fluttering raindrops that flicker like jewels.

Pebbles bathe and glaze with wet colour
    the soil breathes water and steams
the pungent sharpness of bruised roots rises
    grass deepens green and high above me
        young cherries shine red and taut.

I hear water drumming the leaves
    rattling stones, gently sucked down
        earth by low, thirsty spider-web roots.

I put aside the shovel
and inhale slowness.

I can smell the mint and jasmine that will grow here
rust musk of sandalwood dwelling with cedar—
    the scent rubs on my fingers,
        echoing everywhere.

The dirt, pebbles, trees tell me to take my time
as rain shivers and drops as if suspended in air
    as roots follow the low-curved cadence of waiting
and the soaked air brims clouds to a falling fullness;

as long as I'm touching earth I'm planting home

seeding memories, even those that are not my own.

B

Another tongue
    owns me now.

Memories push and pull.
    Refuse to articulate.

Entwined in nets
    of neurons and lobes.

A hope
    that behind
        some locked door
a familiar light
        while dim
still shines.

LANDING

We arrive with our wooden menagerie:
elephants, ducks, mirror-eyed cats and tigers,
the dust of songthaew on our heels
mortar and pestle thoughts in our pockets.

The duck whispers he doesn't like the khanom
farangs eat here and he doesn't eat potatoes.
The painted tigers are frightened of bears.
Even the elephant is scared of mountains.

While in the air the birds tell us nothing,
but we had on thick sweaters and coats
we knew there'd be snow—lots of it!
The cats said so with their mirror eyes.

Outside the Vancouver airport
my father takes a photograph:
        the three of us almost hidden behind our luggage
        meh cradling the rice cooker from Tokyo airport
        my brother amused in a newsboy hat and
        me in a shirt and blue bow-tie, squinting.

Tucked into the southwestern corner
        we don't notice the mountains or sea.
But from the car I see a shirtless boy
        skateboarding on the sidewalk.

The guidebook says we'll be
        offered salmon everywhere—

we'll see.

FIRST DAY

Point to the map

here or there where is here where is

Am I a child of monsoon heat
Am I a child of mountain or sea

It begins when we leave Thailand for
Canada
            saves me from *povertyanddiseaseandignorance*

            (my first English words)

                        oh where oh where is the toilet?
July landing in Vancouver
        a winter coat of orange velveteen
            zipped up ready for snow—

✍

I face the teacher, sitting in a circle.
I am seven and a half years old.
I hear bright feathered blue birds on a red tree.
Suddenly all heads turn to me in a yellow dress
                        she doesn't understand
            she doesn't speak
    English   what is she
            does anyone know   hello hello

                                    (where is the toilet)
Teacher makes all the Asian kids line up
                        try their language on me
not Chinese
            are you sure

                                try again
        definitely not Chinese
                        are you sure
One after another
            they try me:
                        a mystery!
                            (But no one
solves
me)

LESSONS ABOUT CANADA

We were ready to fish for trout
and go skiing every weekend!
We were set to wear parkas,
eat steak and creamed corn!

In the picture I'm in my pink
terry cloth robe and oversized boots
and really there was very little snow
almost none at all
      —but our grins were wide.

"you're in Canada you must look at people in the eye when you talk to them
always say 'yes, please' and 'no, thank you' and always ask for what you want
or you'll never get it speak up speak louder we can't hear you"

I learn not to take rice to school.
      Our home country is
      separated from home.

I learn that it's better to not speak at all.
Vacations and Christmas and Easter
are as foreign to us as we are to them.

We don't celebrate Thai new year
nor the Shan new year either.
But every December 31 we make fruit punch
in a giant crystal bowl from which
little glasses are hung from plastic hooks.

We counted down with the TV.
We raised our cups to the future.
We drew the cups to our lips.

There it was.
The future.

      The future: it tasted
      sweet and sparkling.

LEARNING

Wanting us to be real Canadians
our parents forbid us to speak Thai or Shan.

I remember my tiny tears dripping onto English picture books.
I remember being yelled at for not studying hard enough.
I remember never feeling good enough at eight years old.

My brother is fourteen wearing
      oversized glasses and dad's hand-me-downs.
He clings to his accent until he's nineteen
      when suddenly he loses it as if overnight.
Like how he would miraculously become fluent
      in Italian after four years in Panzano.

Always people asking "Where are you from?"
always assuming we are Chinese or Korean.
We drop our past like we drop stones.
It's almost magic.

I change from Thai to English like I change
clothes and I never look back.
I want to be White.
I want to speak White, look White.
I consumed Whiteness and ate it whole.
The frosting had a sharp sweet edge.

The memory of my first words disappear.
On my lips only English words appear.
but sometimes when I fall asleep

      I hear the vague ghost
      of my own voice speaking Thai and Shan

        but it's a voice I can't quite mimic
        mouth never quite hold.

ENGLISH LESSON

This language gives me life
                         (what have you done
and swallows me up
                         (with the tongue of curves and
                         curlicues
       an insect in a fish on a hook in a fire
       like a gem in a stone in a fist opening

∽

Hey where'dya get your clothes
               hummed air of laundromats

Why does your apartment smell
               immigrant shoes tied-up-to-the-neck shirts
                 (one language subtracts another

Face it you're just nothin' but a refugee
              scuffed jeans from one side of mouth

Whatsa matter cantcha speak English
              (what happened to my face you used to wear

∽

Running after me a Shan girl yelling
     kicking earth,
          can't write but laughs
freely and mocks in tongue
       loose lips wide as my hips in scorn

When I learn my silence she stops   (want
       giggles disappear
knit mouth to tongue   want
        ragged breath in my ear

                     you never get

∽

Do you listen to the rain and imagine it speaking to you?
Do you believe crows call out to you in early morning?

It's a sin to lose the language of your birth
first words so tenderly sung by your cheek
  a dying pant in the ear:
     who are you now but an invasion?

Ghost

That bucking girl
    with the bangs
        sharp sticks in her hand

        listens to the sound of bees
    kicking nectar from flowers and
            licks the salt off rocks

(In the mirror you wanted)

    How the heat
        pushes your head down

    slows your movement   to the pace of clouds

how warmth surrounds like a sleeping cat
        chilies circling its belly

(a different face looking back at you.)

    The first letters   traced in the dirt

        sounds birthed in the throat

    round alphabet   curved vowels

        that cupped your chin and held you so close

Think you can pick up your language like you pick up stones?

Never forget.

I was the first mother
you ran away from.

THE DINNER PARTY

Her made-to-order kitchen spic and span
a you'll damage-the-counter fit to her hand.
At dinner it shows: sliced yellow tomatoes
beaming and gleaming in verdigris oil
grilled eggplant and squash fresh picked
from the farm and local cheese with artisan bread
simple fare rustic fare yeah real farmer food.

The talk is as bounteous as the spread
we're renovating this year
have you been to that Greek island
but we can't seem to find the right help
oh yes in the cave the locals rub you all over
cleaning ladies are so hard
to find yes I love mine but she only does two
houses can't you convince her no she thinks
she's too old and her arthritis you know
well I have at least three people who are looking—

Will they, fascinated, turn to me and ask
where I come from not meaning Vancouver
and I'll have to unfold my long family history
iron out the Canuck version of the American dream
with me as the fairy tale, all educated in my place
really practically one of them what a success story.

Or will they scorn my third world hands
sweep me away as jungle refuse—

Should I offer my services?

I feel double, all tamed animal as I remember
smiling docile nodding at every word
not seething just puzzled at their tunnel-vision talk
perfectly nice people and delightful all that
lucky to have money hired help and cabins on the sly
but for that cash can't see the shadows at their sides
can't see dirt deep in their fingernails
accumulated under the table as
a slant-eyed woman scrubs her bones
down the undersides of their conscience.

Vancouver City Map

The city is articulated
with hand drawn heart
and bent shoe.

George and Simon had a grand ol' time
whistling on ships and powdering wigs
a little blind to some people who were already there
"the town lacked refinement, but it was certainly lively."

In 1886 it was named.
Three months later,
it burned down.

Thus began a history
of ugly incidents.

The city wants me.

I weave up escalators through
the closed eyelids of the morning.
All of it drains from us, the exhaust, the spitting,
the voices, the hands thrusting newspapers,
the chores of the day, the tapping, the emails,
trying to remember where all the time went.

&

On the SkyTrain
heavy heads nod like
punch-drunk boxers.

Brightness, brightness,
over the lip of the mountain.
Pink hands, pink cheeks,
pink sky.

When you are in such an ambidextrous city

you are likely to lose your way.
One must be careful not to enter territory that one is unaccustomed to,

lest you haphazardly intrude on an imagination that wishes to remain
private.

(1792)

George was surprised to meet
a Spanish explorer while
discovering the new land

and "mortified" to learn that
another Spaniard had
landed a year before him

(but somehow wasn't too
bothered by the people
who were already here)

he straightened his wig.
Galiano, ol' buddy,
there's nothing a little
rum won't fix, hmmm?

(1886)

Ah, city of exponential growth!
Ah, what worlds oceans bring!
The port is sorted, the ships sing.

In the grocer's display window
the asses of upturned deer become
improvised vases when stuffed
with bouquets of azaleas;
green bananas hang from the ceiling—
so much Klondike dust on our fingers.
Step up, step in here with dogs, mules, pickaxes
harnesses, leather gloves and teaspoons,
grimy boots, dirty fists and the smell
of felled 1,000-year-old cedars.

Let's play the game of speculation, folks!
land passes from pocket to pocket—
just hold on till the prices rise!
Now ain't this a pretty plot full
of trees, and hey, they're buildin'
that new hotel 'cross the way
so empty and majestic, this land
yours for the talkin' and takin'.

Towering certainties
of mirrored high-rises.
Mountains nudging the city
into the sea.

Glass and metal:
    the dark sky of rain.

Impartial, never the streets
umbrellas point up

        What little tigers
     stalk the faces of—

Sockeye return

> by miracle
>> or mystery

Scientists announce their astonishment
and fishermen proclaim the getting
hasn't been this good in 50 years.

> Nets unravel into ocean.
Flashes of scarlet nose the fighting river
as factories reopen for perfect killing.

Long ago, they say fish were so plentiful
you could reach into the sea and
catch one with your bare hands.

Those were the stories.

Anyway.

(1914)

Ahoy, ahoy, no welcome mat for you
that's what happens when you don't read
the fine print, why don't you people ever learn?
Boys, my brightly turbaned boys, when we say
DIRECT we mean DIRECT we don't care if
you stopped in—where?—Hong Kong
for 2 seconds, see it says "DIRECTLY from
the place of origin" Why, everyone round here
comes from someplace except for them over there.
Now, those ladies and gents, they came DIRECT
from ol' England, you see? Now we've got that
outta the way, how's about a game of cards, boys?

Broken umbrellas, shards of glass, plumes of
bright plastic, soiled candy wrappers line the
concrete like hieroglyphics on the street.
The stench of rot, vomit, and piss—
the alley is woozy with it.

(1889)

The bear thrust
its fat mitt
into the giant
tree hollow
its silver chain
umbilical.

The park ranger
with the moustache
and the shackle
to the grand
cedar stump.

His interest was
purely zoological

Mr. Black Bear,
he giggled,
meet Mr. Blackberry.

As we move away from Stanley Park
forests muddle, green patches
slash alongside grey buildings—

Coffee is always hot
Words strange in your mouth—

point to the 'place of articulation'

on every corner a coffee shop

Word is the code for the thing
we have a code for the
code:

you hesitate to name the heart.

(1887)

Under the great Canadian steel back bone,
under the weep blasted rock and gold dust,
under the bloodied candied rust of dirt,
  more bones
        more bones
     piled like
           dominoes.
∾

Oh, Engine No. 374,
     how Continental, how National!

(1922)

Seraphim Joe, Seraphim Joe,
Bajan feet and sugarcane blood
do you blink, see Mount Hillaby
rise like a grey whale, all scarred and slick
a conjuring trick, your swimming kick

bending the long genuine length of ocean
silver and blue fish reddening your ears
every arm stroke a life saved, a life lived
as porter, handyman, bartender, a West End
man born from a shipwreck and beach brown neck

Seraphim Joe, Seraphim Joe,
no family, only wet white-gloved smiles
yet yellow eyes peck at your squat gold watch
the Carib Grackle folds its black wings
in your ear that tickita-tickita-tickita-ting.

This game is a game of exhaustion

a dizzying game, with no end in sight.

The game requires every player's full participation.

The rules must be agreed upon by the players.

(1885)

Mountains burden our eyes.
Rocks are too heavy for our arms,
we are the people of paper.

We shrugged off our sun drenched
skins imbedded with market smells
emerging white, glittering and icy.

We are so pure.

We are spectres on the chess board.

There is no square for us.

⋖

People walk with memories
of all the homes they lived in.

Some still dream of footfalls on their streets,
a land that only exists in memory
(did it ever exist at all?)

Some words still foreign to the mouth
even after so many years.

When looking at a map
position is important.

Align yourself to a particular landmark,
become extension to the city in which you are lost.

Prepositions are less important,
whether you are on or in some place.

Near a historical building you might find
an immovable map, itself a statue

and strangely, as in a Borges story
you meet yourself through plexiglass:

discover the ideolocator—an arrow, a dot—
saying "You are here."

The city is new and ever in its newness.

High-rises creep closer to shore.

Glass is our emblem.

It reveals and always reflects.

We break up an immense
city into villages.

We want smallness.

Somehow, the city has raised us
to identify a babel of languages.

I was born in a tropical country
but flew across the ocean
to settle near a powerful river.

I live in a house carved in
the slope of a mountain.
Voices cross and sing.
Thoughts tick and tock.

The rain falls.
The fog lifts.

Downtown, footsteps follow each other.
Trolley buses throw minute sparks
into a buffet of clouds.

Strangers sit together, huddled
in communion of steam and chopsticks
over fragrant bowls of ramen
broth golden and dotted with fat.

C

      The electricity
I create
    is small.

      Grief and love
have similar beginnings
         but indistinct ends.

(The heart
    breaks
upriver.)

      Await an answer—
hide my wounds
        in the fissures
   of the world.

UNDER MY TONGUE

Is a world which laughs
Is a country where grass grows
        a million miles high

There is a tree which carries
volcanoes on its branches very tip
in leaves of rubies and sapphires.

Tamarind and lychee fruits
                launch from my fingers.

My bed is amongst the rice paddies
enclosed by the scent of jasmine.

Under my tongue
        rivals the tropical jungles
in its diversity of many strange things.

Under my tongue
        is an immense ocean
                larger than the breadth of the Pacific.

When the waves
hit my teeth
        vowels rolls in its waters
        words splash out.

Beware.

Under my tongue
        is a word
                deadly as a dart
that can pierce someone's heart.

Way Blood Travels

From my grandmother
                    I inherit cravings
            for intense sour

At the age of three she feeds me tart red fruits
mashed with salt and nampla
I crave green mangoes dipped in salt
pickled gooseberries green plums in brine

                    Think of sour and mouth
                                    wells

My mother is known for spices
                    fingers plunged in coriander
her intense Shan flavours
            magic ginger thumb touches everything

And in Italy before a small gas stove
                    I find myself missing home
nursing her in the stir of pots
            and the tastes come out
vaguest cooking techniques suddenly   appear
measure by instinct
                            fingertip improvisation
of tongue trained in Shan Burmese Thai
            cooking through   rolls in the mouth
                    her in my bones urging curried potatoes out

                    tomatoes whirl about
orange tinged rice   lemon salad

        Crisp fried onion flakes fall into

                            bowls

        How does the body know   or

                                    how does it forget

PANZANO

(A Poem in Voices)

Here, hills roll with the sea
the land rises, overlapping hills
an endlessness like the ocean,
rows on rows of vineyards flow into
curved terraces of olive groves,
sun in those bright leaves
grapes imprinting purple and dark
as winds flip through sprawling vines,
as all the fields gather sunlight
waving warmth and yellow
and deep bright gold.

                    I come to the land which gathered you
                    in its arms from frostbitten Canada

                    I come to Italy stomach queasy
                    curving as the bus turns up mountains
                    but I look and for the first time in my life
                    I can't quite believe what I see

Black roosters invade the piazza
shiny eyes painted, wooden combs flaming.
Three-wheeled Apis sputter up curves
as BMWs lurch hurriedly up the hills, rushing
for market day where vans spill open to sell
dried arm-length sausages flecked with fat
barrel-sized cheeses sitting like white
bellies on crates alongside fish
jewelled in salt their stenches elbowing
the aroma of whole roasted pigs their skins
crackly and pocked with bubbles
roasted chicken turning clear juices running,
a layer of grease lines the day as people clutch
parchment bags of deep-fried polenta
fingers transparent with fat and oil.

A red-lipped woman tries on shapely boots
while a brown-skinned foreigner
gestures at toys in broken Italian.

Tall young men command street corners in threes
heads thrown back
ready to caw.

Is it possible for a person to swallow the whole land?
To take it everywhere, like a talisman.
Fingertips. The long valley of the back.

did you run away
too in love with art

all my life I've followed you
your colours spread before me
follow follow

Autumn enters the narrow streets
its sides rubbing against stone walls
rounding angles of pink rock
winding through unpaved roads
sloping uphill and down, curving
round slopes and circles of the land
it plays with the wind on its tongue,
opening its mouth wide and
in a breath of cold
pushes the sun farther away.

he doesn't believe in metaphors

your small body crying over a book
nothing was ever good enough
dad's anger so hard pummeling whatever was left
years later my brother you long to disappear
aim for the west run after the sun
something in you pushing stronger than his hands

Earth work:
the spine pulls back
as the old man bends to pick
up a rock with gravel-rough fingers,
the dry and hollow joints
rattling inside his tanned skin.

He chases the ground,
searching for shapes—
a delicate task, choosing
a stone that would fit.
He sniffs the air; he can smell
cold coming, even in this sun.
He feels it in his fingers too:
they begin to ache for olives.

haven't had a dream in a long time
yellow crocus under the hand

In this sloped forest
trees stand at odd angles
curved toward
then away
from the ground.

Stories are passed hand to hand.
Like stones. Like seaweed breaking a water's surface.

you surprise me when you say you feel at home in this foreign land
you who always felt the difference in our skin our slit eyes here more alien
as I walk on cobbled stones of the village I can't help but feel eyes in walls
it must be instinct but I look for brown faces
dark eyes that don't belong

What tourists don't see is
whispered in the deserted piazza
in the slow aimless shuffle of old men
corduroy caps soft and sagging

hooks of withered hands
wrestling crooked canes;
in the bodies of women moving
with quick efficiency, arms
hung heavy with raw meat.

Are we bones already?

Trees surround him.
He hears nothing, except the sharp
gritty spread of mortar on rock.

His gnarled hands, chapped and flaking
rest on cool moss; rain already
on the ground before it has fallen;
his knees sunk in the earth know it.
He moves quicker, scraping away
mortar with the trowel, picks up
another piece, moving from tree to tree.

dear holy blessed virgin please don't let it rain today
dear mother you have witnessed the efforts of these old hands amen

Old trees, bark, lichen and cold sweat,
trunks twisted and curved like immense vines
stoop to touch each other.

Do you believe in God? By the palm of your hand I see you have been writ
upon. Here by your thumb the moment of your birth; this line is when you die.
An oak tree on your hand—here are the stars, the constellations that you must live by.
Forget the moon.

A woman wakes up in the middle of the night.
Dreamed when her belly was stretched white,
her belly the moon, heavy and pulling down.
In dream she stands before an open window,

warm wind rasping, night running down her body.
Before her the moon, sliced naked.
She closes her eyes.
Before her the moon blossoms into roundness,
pouring out light which shimmers
encircling dark like handless waving fingers.

release me gently to the night
when shadow and air become indistinct
when we turn our backs to the day
when nothing we gesture to remains;
only press my eyelids closed with your lips
so I can no longer see
but the shape of your breath,
but the indecipherable lines of your lips,
but the heat from your mouth gliding
when signs dissolve we breathe together
and suddenly find stars on our skin

Boar hunting season.
Blade-sharp quills dripping musk
The sound of shotgun splinters
scorched gunpowder stings his snout
nowhere nowhere
crippled trees circle like prey.

rain will bring night and night will come crawling through the holes

he picks me up by the side of the road
offers a ride back to town I'm grateful
my pack is heavy shoulders pins in them
non parlo italiano non parlo italiano
even though I don't understand he keeps talking
one hand moves towards my breasts the language
lunging between my legs I push his hand away
and again we're moving we're moving up the hill so slowly
can't get out I want to jump out of the car no no no *cinquantemillelire*
again his one hand reaching the other on the wheel *cinquantemillelire*
I can't believe my ears but I'm too scared
to tell him fuck off or scream or do anything

car so small the air disappears
when we reach the piazza in sight of the *polizia*
he laughs it off slaps my shoulder and says *scherzo*: joke

is there an order to the earth

Wind a heated beast
rubbing its fur against your skin
wind hot flannel on a lover's body
wind warm water running you over.

Today the wind is wild
warm wind from Morocco
bursting November in flames.

chili on his tongue
red in his belly
cinnamon skin

Sam from Sri Lanka, now a handyman
invites us over to see his wife and brand new baby
he offers us orange Fanta in his apartment all vinyl tablecloth
plastic folding chairs but the place is orderly trying for a sense of home

we are the only brown people in this town
all in one tiny room
and I remember how the four of us
shared a one-bedroom apartment
when we first came to Canada

well Sam's grinning and his wife is laughing as
they unveil the little girl infant they name:
Los Angeles

Miles from here the Tuscan hills
stretch smooth and flat and long;
tall, thin grasses grow bright green
catch the warmth, play the light.
A wind comes, pushing the stalks
down, up, until the sun shines everything

yellow like it'd been dipped in ghee.

A large cloud lumbers over the sky
shading the ground and green
becomes dark, blue overcomes
the wide field, colours flapping,
and sudden he sees before him the ocean.

Through beaming cloud-gaps
light sprinkles the land silver
and everything is waves, is water,
as a choked laugh comes out
of his throat as he sees his dreams
for the first time as he sees
for the last time his home.

I'm confused by my wanting
anger and punishment and revenge

I'm afraid to go out
without someone by my side

body so heavy
I come with pitch
dark rhythm
imagine me
imagine slowly

you say how sad I am all the time
you're angry for me but no one knows
the anger at myself so spineless and weak
it's almost a lesson: to be reminded
the dangers of being an Asian woman

you ask me what he looks like but
don't remember don't remember

Fruits rot on trees

walnuts blacken the ground
figs slump and collapse from within
scorched grapes wither into folds
apples bleed the ground.

a cold scab the sun
light no longer divides the thick
air grown white and shivering

Through the window the first smoke
he remembers walking between trees
smelling like sandalwood for day.

Shaded in tree-shadow
soil breathes in wet
the undergrowth
of mauve gentians and yellow mushrooms
is coated with the deep shiver of earth.

Autumn brings the smell of fire
as fruits sprawl stinking
vineyards blaze, smoke
darkens the church.

All the dogs howl and bark
as the air grows cold and dark
grey dark clouds have wings
swiftly crossing the sky to bring
the scent of rain combined with fire.

The night grows blacker
stars are not seen
an orange moon fills the eyes

Streets are bare, even old men stay away.

The air is overcome, a white sky overwhelms.
Cobblestones suck in wet as the air drinks trees pale.
Wind slows. Sun deadens.
Drenched chill in every breath.

Then, with stand-still swiftness,
clouds crowd in, yoking dark upon dark
twisting day into night as a sturdy wind rises
pulling at cypresses which lean confusedly
as it hurls down the last stubborn apples
wind an icy flood gusting with great screams
contorting freezing rain which shatter like glass;
it shoves windows open, knocking over
potted plants on windowsills
smashing open baked red clay
and scattering wet earth.

one night you're late from the gallery and we wait
telephone rings and something's happened
car accident everyone is fine but knee banged up pretty bad

your wristwatch at the moment of impact has stopped

When he was born everything
was made of water, in his mind ocean
undulating blue, the air moss
breaths dew-filled, waters wide and wide.

I will leave here soon
and fly over the Atlantic
leaving you to your European mysteries

you have come here to be unambiguous, I think
to be an exile, a forever foreigner in white eyes

Canada is too ambivalent for your nature
too hurtful in its half-hearted welcoming

alone among the trees in the tiny forest

I stare at tree trunks
eyes rumble around the earth;
flowers surprised in green nests
reach for earth
my hand touches
every minute thing

Drenched clouds hang on boughs
air quivers with rain fallen and gone;
plush undergrowth gleam in shade
as tree trunks anchor in sloped earth.

This forest an odd patch of land
belonging to itself, away from town:
a refuge of warped trees.

Large trunks have gaping mouths
hollowed by a sickness:
red and black ashes coat the cavities
and dark craters reach up and up.

The smell of dankness and rotting.
The damp smell of trees dying.

An astonishment:
at the base of the trunks
mortared stones fill the diseased cavities.
Trees natural, half-human.

The walls now fit so well stones
become bark, trunk, tree.

But the time, the care of this act,
crouching before a near-collapsed form
hands reading the striations of bark
feeling for flaking muscles of wood.

Long hours of skin against moss
knees in black dirt
stacking stones.

Even as winter approaches

trees tall lean and still
 budded in green
 leaves birthing pebbly acorns.

At once living and dying.

Falling and ascending.

Branches that jut left suddenly twist right:

 eerie trapezoids against a gently blue sky.

SALT CRUST FISH

In a Bangkok restaurant stall
we break the thick salt crust.
For the first time you speak
about the "Lady" and your
doubts about Burma and the cause.

True leaders are hard to come by.
This is implied.
The country has
a cement future.

Next to us a thin young man sits quietly,
six empty litre bottles of Chang beer on his table.
We pick bones from the carp.

It surprised me that we never fought.
The memory of you as my father,
fierce and angry and disappointed at us,
I suppose, sat inside me, silently in dread.
Each day you went to the conference
and always came back weary, tired
for your lost country, your 40-year exile.

From the road-side food stalls we
buy charcoal-grilled squid skewers
placed in plastic bags and poured
over with nam jim, khao neow.
We go back to the hotel room
and eat with bare fingers.

You were always trying to get me
outside, see wats, the tourist sights.

But after weeks of travelling alone
I felt more lonely around people
than I ever did shut up in a hotel room.
All I wanted was the air-conditioned air
the enclosed feeling of familiar streets
and that feeling of safety, of home.

A Homecoming

They imagined the house
matchstick to matchstick.
Arranged windows like jigsaw pieces
striped walls with the hue of their skin.

Birds with yellow eyes
Lent their black wings to bless
the flat roof, and with spiny feet
gingerly tested the shiny wood floors.

For Loi Krathong we perch thin
white candles along the windows
and the porch, the iron fence.
Fire budding like winter flowers.

When we left, we gave away
the furniture and our calico cats.
The paint still smelled new
floors still felt fur smooth.

᷒

I return twenty years later,
an elephant in a doll's house.

Chiang Mai flexed, crowed and crowded close,
corrugated tin roofs overhang like bent elbows.

The tip of my head and giant arms
threaten to crack the ceiling.

The walls closed in with cramped
betrayal, each room diminished and thin.

Our avian godmothers flew off years ago.
The cats have run away, searching in the dirt for lost things.
Plants have ballooned to a wildness and a deep green looms over.
The house repainted a sparse blue, dust in the corners.

THAI SUITES

A bungalow cabin with plastic walls
300 baht a night and the fan full on.
The air drips thickly with wet heat and
far away, the waving ocean, moving over
bright hot sands, and outside the window
the squish and squeeze of water as two girls
wash and wring clothes with their hands.

At night in Hua Hin, bloated white-haired men
hang on to their young Thai girlfriends
hooks around their slight stems.

❧

36°C, the rain arrives after darkness
watery feet over the thin roofs
banging the thick, green leaves, making
sidewalks dark, damp-smelling and fresh
as if the streets were new again.

In the morning a fox-nosed dog,
teats pulled and hanging down,
drinks out of mirrored puddles.

❧

"BS Bakery"

"UN Enterprises"

"Know-You Seed Co. Ltd."

Signs passed by on the train

(I thirst for English here)

✍

In the spotless Loei hotel room
I find critters: shiny-helmeted ants
trudging on the melamine nightstand.
A cockroach the size of a pocket watch
falls, like Icarus, from the air-conditioner.
A miniature green frog hops into the room.

Like a royal attendant I usher
him out into the courtyard.

✍

On the bus ride to Chiang Rai
the roads are curved, like letters from
the bows and arches of the Thai alphabet.
I'm surprised at how bright red the dirt is

almost like I'm asleep and
Thailand is a dream.

✍

From the morning market in Ayutthaya
I buy 2 kilos of rhambutan and mangosteen
but I get lost and wander for two hours
finding streets that aren't on the map
or streets with only names in Thai.

I give up and hire a motorcycle taxi
a bag of fruit hanging from each arm
feet dangling, exhaust blasting, as we
weave around cars and songthaews.

✍

I don't talk to travellers at the guest house
but then no one talks to me either, 'cause for
some reason they think I don't speak English
or think I'm one of the Thai workers in the back.

Anyway they all seem to be coming back from the beach
wrapped in white towels, empty bottles of water in hand.We speak the

same language but
seem to come from different worlds.

Laughing and loud
bright and shining
seeing the world through
dark-glassed eyes.

The wife of the songthaew driver
smiles and says her English
name is "Moon," but in Thai
it's "Deun," meaning "to walk."

She offers me pieces of deep fried
chicken skin from her paper bag
and says I look like a Thai from
Chiang Mai, "pretty, white skin"
our voices on thin stilts
languages halved and broken—

✍

At a market in northeast Issan province
a smiling woman in bright sarongs offers me
a piece of jackfruit, yellow and warm from the sun
in my mouth the firm winey honey sweetness
and I buy a big bag of the fruit, peeled
from its green, small mediaeval points.

In that city I eat the most delicious som tam,
studded with bright red chilies like firecrackers
My stomach rumbles but it's so good
that fermented saltiness and lime—

✍

       Twins everywhere

On a Thai variety TV show a competition
between different sets of twins: one plays saxophones,
another set shares a single guitar and another performs
a muscular striptease, complete with sailor hats and navy suits.
Not sure what the prize was, but usually it's just
a bag of fat lychees or some 3000 baht or so

In the news today, the Siamese twins born joined at the head
dies after the surgery to separate them

>>> 90 minutes apart
>>>>>> when they were apart

∽

To worry is to "mai jai,"
>>> or "burn heart"

Tears is "nam dtaa,"
>>> or "water eye"

Compassion is "nam jai,"
>>> or "water heart"

∽

Lost again
>>> lost again

>>> After visiting the internet café in Khampaeng Phet
I try to get back to the guest house, but spend
hours wandering half empty streets

>>> Stray dogs and fenced houses
>>> everywhere I turn there's barking
>>>>>> a brown poodle and a terrier chase me
>>>>>>>>> nipping at my pant legs

Finally I spot an old man driving
>>> a scooter with cart in front
>>> Frantically gesturing, I get a ride
>>>>>> balancing between bags of rice

∽

>>> The Buddha Chinnarat sits as if soaked in morning
>>> gold that shines and softens like a feathered sun
>>> Spires arise from his body, rising he sits
>>> softly smiling as if in the middle of flames

Later I learn how to catch fish
with a small trap of thorns

Walking by the dark green Nan River I see
a hundred middle-aged men and women
in red and blue and yellow sweatsuits
moving arms legs in aerobic unison
to the wild blasting electronic beat of
Kylie's "Can't Get You Out of My Head"

∽

A room with a bed
and a ceiling fan

empty plastic bottles of water all in a row.
The white linoleum floor.

The day's discards,
pages of Bangkok Post
scattered on the bed.
I remember at the airport gate
looking back at my parents
realizing how much older they've gotten,
and feeling, for the first time,
that one day, they too will die.

I miss the cold.
I miss the evergreens.
I miss having four walls that know me.

It's surprising
that I long so
for home here,

my Canada.

Inside My House

I find a tremendous secret
inside the curl of seashells,
in the cracked pit of a peach.

Silent like the tear ducts of my eyes,
I stay coiled like a newborn snake.
There is nothing I need.

For entertainment I watch
the tug-of-war between
an elephant and a hundred men.

I have costumes for the hot season,
the rainy season and the cool season.
The King changes my costumes himself.

I don't want to be seen,
to have voices address me.
This is what I have wanted, always.

My teeth are strong.
I keep them as sharp
as the fingernails of tigers.

No one knows that there are
390 steps to my house, and
sometimes it is very cold there.

GLEANING STONES

We walk the path
between water, sand, stone
grey waves continually licking
never wishing for sifted southern sands
never for the swelling air of flowered heat.

Side by side, papa and I
feet nudged by cold water cold wind
sea water intensifying pebble colours
looking down broken by joyful lurches
silently dropping stones into pockets
waves grazing rock
lapping sand.

He disappears quickly
inside a split rock
in that touch between
water and wave

I stand alone on the shore.

✺

    Look
this egg-shaped stone:
      the colour of newborn grass
        skin of a tight orange.

See this pebble, flat and round
      the size of three fingertips squeezed together
     being black crow feather alighted by the sun
      smooth as inner thigh skin.

A red square stone the length of a thumb:
     touch spilt-open ridged end to end
      like thick blood.

A stone for your silence
a stone in your throat
the first clutching stone,
the hole in your eye
in the year of your death.

Over the shoulder and into the sea,
bandages are removed from your head.
Bloodied skin and bruised stapled smile.
Stones of fire, no wish will come.

Passed hand to hand,
the stone in your brain
cannot speak to your eroding body.
A stone to the heart.

A collection of stones
and no metallic hope.
Stones your beginning and your end.
Your future a cut skull.

Papa, dear papa
stones under my bed
and under my pillow
stones in the fountain:
your life for a stone.

A Troubled Sleep

The beach is lonely in early morning:
        bull kelp, barnacles and bits of broken shell.
Shy ankles ease into the Pacific.
The river is never far away.

I think of Forché's angel always looking back,
        witnessing deaths by force and accident,
        wars, bombings and shootings
        viewed through the debris of history.
        She must be sad all the time.

                I think of Burma.
                I think of Canada.
                Clockwork of ocean
                waves that beat time.

I keep away the lullaby of the waters.
I keep a troubled sleep.

I think: the sea will always be.
We have our certainties.

I do not believe we will drown in the waters.
Heads bowed into the night, uncertain of dark.
The future crawls frightened
into holes in the floor.

The horizon is somewhere
        we want to go to but can never go.
At night, the seas are mirrors
        for lights from glass buildings.

Waters suffuse with moonlight and electricity.
Such depths, such mysteries we don't know.

Waters tangled like bed sheets between our legs.
We wait for a terrifying promise that has yet to come.

SHORE

Air falls in slate.
The sea is sharp and chipped
blades gleaming in a cold light.

Granite precipices crouch
along the North Shore
hulking against wet horizon.

My sweater opens—

❧

Last night I dream of drowning.
People gone away do not return.
The eyes of the man
who teaches beauty
are overwhelmed by clouds.

❧

I'm startled by the carcass of a fish
its eyes eaten away
mouth opened wide.

A seagull perches on the tail
pulling at pink flesh
its wings pushing and flapping.

The fish seems
to be grinning.

❧

I clamber over crags
yellowed seaweed
molar-like barnacles.

Tiny mussels fused with blue
cling in razor-edged clumps.

❧

That moment when
your brain stopped
putting letters together.
How words became
a handful of prickly
disparate rocks.

You'd sit in front
of the computer.
Frowning in concentration
staring at the screen
typing the same random
letters over and over.

❧

Gathering stones:
a childhood habit.

But even the brightest stones dim
collected on a windowsill
amongst dead things.

❧

I understand now
the headstone
that marks where
a human body once lay.

❧

The fish is born
swallowed by the throat of the sea.

The fish
swallowed by the bird
takes flight over the waves.

❧

Below waves shatter
gathering and battering rocks.

❧

In those
last days

you made
breathing
seem like the
hardest
thing.

❧

The morning
drained of light

gathers the wind and cloud
in its great overcoat and dark pockets.

WE FOLLOW THE RIVER

Nurses tip you over as if
you were filled with oceans.
They swaddle your hollow hips in
cloth and plastic, utter whiteness.

The hospital's patch of grass is
worn down by back and forth.
Your bed is too bright—
do you ever remember snow falling?

No one quite knew about you
or how much time you had.
In your brain a stem
that doesn't flower.

The air become as mouths
that are forever swallowing.
Some days you remember us.
Most days you don't speak at all.

Outside the SkyTrain slices
cleanly into the blue horizon.
The new station like a human spine,
metal rafters grey and skeletal.

The day we sat by your empty
urn we sat on stones,
pant cuffs wet with river.

So many stories will never be complete now.

You died, not peacefully like a river
but gasping like a hot ocean.

We follow the Fraser, the sun
bending water in brindled fingerprints.
Fish are invisible under such light.

In the distance they are making new
mountains out of steel and glass now.

NOTES

"Vancouver City Map" was initially published as an artist's hand-made chapbook by fish magic press in 2016 in a limited edition of 38 copies.

"1886" — the new city of Vancouver was formed on April 6, 1886. Almost the entire city was destroyed three months later on June 13 in a large fire.

"ahoy" — this poem refers to the steamer *Komagata Maru*, which carried 376 passengers from India on May 23, 1914. They were refused entry because of a 'continuous journey' restriction, which maintained that all immigrants must come to Canada directly from their country of origin, without stopping.

"the bear" — Henry Avison was Stanley Park's first park superintendent, and started what turned out to be the beginnings of a zoo when he captured and kept a black bear chained to a tree stump.

"under the great Canadian steel backbone" — The first CPR train to arrive in Vancouver was Engine number 374, on May 23, 1887.

"Seraphim Joe" — Seraphim "Joe" Fortes is a renowned man in Vancouver history, known for being the first appointed lifeguard in Vancouver's English Bay, and teaching numerous children to swim. For his service to the city he was given, among other things, a gold watch.

Earlier versions of poems were published in anthologies and journals. "A Homecoming" and "We Follow the River" were published in *The New Quarterly* (Issue 115, 2010), and "We Follow the River" was later anthologized in *The Best Canadian Poetry in English 2011* (Tightrope Books); it was also included in *Force Field: 77 Women Poets of British Columbia* (Mother Tongue Publishing, 2013), along with "First Day" and "Her, Cooking." "Way Blood Travels" was first published in the anthology *Portfolio Milieu* (Sumach Press, 2004) and later published in the anthology *Poems from Planet Earth* (Leaf Press, 2013). "English Lesson" was published in the anthology *Rocksalt: An Anthology of Contemporary BC Poetry* (Mother Tongue Publishing, 2008). "Inside My House" and "Gleaning Stones" were published in *The Maynard* (Spring 2017). The "Seraphim Joe" excerpt from "Vancouver City Map" was published in *subTerrain: Vancouver 125* (2011). An early version of "Vancouver City Map" was published in Sugar Mule #29 (2008). "My Mother's Hands" was previously published in *Room*

32.3 (2009). "Thai Suites" was published in *Ricepaper* 14.1 (2009). Earlier versions of "Moving Earth" were published in *Grain* 29.2 (2001) and later anthologized in *4 Poets* (Mother Tongue Publishing, 2009). Versions of "Green Mango," "First Day" and "Under My Tongue" were published in the anthology *Portfolio Milieu* (Sumach Press, 2004).

Acknowledgements

This book is dedicated to my father, Chao Tzang, who died in 2004, and my mother, Nu Nu, who passed away in 2022. Their lives as Shans were at times fraught, dangerous, and risky, all in the fight for freedom for an independent Burma/Myanmar. I only knew them as they were in Canada, when we were poor and struggling, and how each of us tried in our own way to make this country a home. Like many children, I had a myopic view of who my parents were and only began to conceive of them as autonomous, independent human beings when I was an adult. It struck me all of a sudden how courageous they were to leave Thailand and come to Vancouver, how tragedy had struck their lives just at the time of blooming, how they were forced to endure all that came after. Their lives weren't perfect, nor were they perfect people.

I've been writing this book for over twenty years. Most of the poems were first written when I was in my early twenties, when I was a very different person. The manuscript has been worked on and put away repeatedly over the decades. I was never happy with it. It is even fair to say that I had given up hope for it. This past year, soon after my mother died, I looked over the manuscript. So many of these poems were about her. It seemed time to put the poems out into the world. The poems were then revised, over and over, until the present me was satisfied (a rather daunting task). In this work, I hope that my younger self and present self are united in some harmonious way.

To Vici, Sarah, Malaika and the team at Caitlin Press: thank you for your hard work and enthusiasm.

Thanks to my early writing mentors who provided feedback on poems from this book: Betsy Warland, Warren Cariou, Marilyn Dumont. Huge thanks to Mona Fertig and Bill New for first taking a chance on my work.

Grateful for the decades-long friendship with Travis V. Mason, who is both kind and astute in his literary insights. Infinite thanks to Hazel Jane Plante for being a brilliant editor, writer, long-time creative collaborator and for being the best, most supportive friend.

To the A-Team: Natalie Ord, Karen Estrin, Jean Parlina, Brianna Spicer, and Vi Nguyen. You are the most witty, intelligent, lovely group of strong women. I adore you.

Gratefulness and love to Cristina Pangilinan, Brigid O'Regan, Chantal Gibson, Baharak Yousefi, Daniela Elza, who have always supported me and my writing endeavors.

A thousand thanks to Joel DeStefano for his friendship, joyous creative energy, and intelligence.

Thanks to all the Yawnghwe family, especially the Montreal branch of Samara, Keharn, Harn and Helen. Thank you to Sanda Simms, a writing role model since I was a child.

Finally: endless love to Sawan, Kris, Indira, Django and Mudra. And to Elai, Ekow, Ramona, Pique, and Aggie: darling feline companions, past and present.

ABOUT THE AUTHOR

Onjana Yawnghwe is a Shan-Canadian writer and illustrator who lives in the traditional, ancestral, and unceded lands of the Kwikwetlem First Nation. She is the author of two poetry books, *Fragments, Desire* (Oolichan Books, 2017) and *The Small Way* (Dagger Editions 2018), both of which were nominated for the Dorothy Livesay Poetry Prize. She works as a registered nurse. Her current projects include a graphic memoir about her family and Myanmar, and a book of cloud divination.